Half Yard
Christmas

Half Yard
Christmas

Debbie Shore

Easy sewing projects using
left-over pieces of fabric

SEARCH PRESS

First published in 2015

Search Press Limited
Wellwood, North Farm Road,
Tunbridge Wells, Kent TN2 3DR

Reprinted 2015

Photographs by Garie Hind
Styling by Kimberley Hind
Monochrome model: Kimberley
Contemporary models: Maria and Dior
Scandinavian model: Hettie
Traditional model: Sadie
Kids models: Sadie and Elise

ISBN: 978 1 78221 147 1

Suppliers
For details of suppliers, please visit the
Search Press website: www.searchpress.com

Printed in China

Acknowledgements

Thank you to the team at Search Press,
who I think have enjoyed working on my
books as much as I have!

We try to produce quality, inspiring
books with my words, my husband
Garie's photography and Search Press'
beautiful presentation, with ideas from
all sides. I hope you enjoy them as
much as we do.

Contents

Introduction

When I was a child, Christmas was always home-made. I remember sprinkling multi-coloured glitter over pencil drawings of reindeer and snow scenes, and gathering layers of lace to make a skirt for the tree fairy. The too-long scarf my sister knitted for me, which I thought I'd cleverly trim with scissors… the snowman ornament with the springy neck that stretched over the years so that his head rested quizzically on his shoulder. Snowballs, choirs, roast dinner and Christmas pudding, trying so hard to sleep on Christmas Eve but so wanting to hear sleigh bells and Santa's ho-ho-ho, then running downstairs at an unearthly hour to see if the stockings were filled with Christmas treats. We forget much of our childhood, but Christmas is remembered with such warmth. No matter what your style or choice of decoration is, I'm hoping that this book will help you to create the memorable Christmases for your family that I experienced with my own.

Christmas is celebrated in many different styles, from the traditional reds and greens with halls decked in holly, to the simple reds and whites of Nordic décor and the rustic charm of natural fibres. I'm hoping the projects in this book will inspire you and help you to add a touch of personality and character to any room you decorate.

The fabrics I've used are all woven cottons, with felt for the kids' section, and no fancy sewing machine required! A straight stitch is the only one needed for most of these projects, and I've used a ¼in (0.5cm) seam allowance unless stated otherwise. Of course you can choose whatever fabrics you like in any colour scheme that suits your room. Hopefully this book will give you a bit of inspiration and the confidence to have a go!

Debbie

Tools & equipment

The projects in this book are easy for a beginner to make, therefore the tools and equipment needed are quite basic.

Sewing machine: I've only used a straight stitch for these projects so you don't need anything fancy, but if you want to do free-motion embroidery you'll need a machine with a drop feed dog facility.

Free-motion embroidery foot: this is used for stippling your quilted projects and 'doodling' with thread on projects like the ribbon tree placemats (see pages 116–117). The machine shown top right has an embroidery foot in place.

Repositionable spray adhesive: make sure it's suitable for fabric – adhesive for paper won't be good for your sewing machine.

Bamboo creaser: perfect for turning out corners, as in the rustic wreath parcels (see page 34), the bamboo creaser has a rounded end so it won't tear your corners, and the flat side can be used to crease open seams instead of pressing. Shown right.

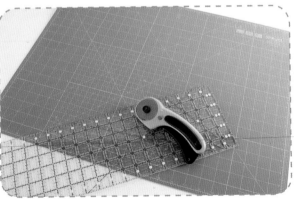

Rotary cutter, rectangular ruler and mat: these three go together, and quite simply I use them to cut anything straight! They give real accuracy both in cutting straight lines and measuring – they are absolute must-haves. There are useful 45-degree angles on the ruler and the mat, to make cutting bias strips a doddle, and they are available in inches and centimetres – sometimes both. The mats are self-healing and I would advise you to go for the largest you can. The most popular size for a rotary cutter is 45mm. Shown right.

Scissors: long, sharp dressmakers' scissors are an important tool for precision cutting. Keep a small pair of scissors for snipping threads and detailed cutting.

Bias tape maker: this is a handy little tool for creating creased bias strips, and the most used size is 1in (2.5cm). Cut bias strips of fabric to 2in (5cm) wide, pull through the tool and press with a hot iron as it comes out. Mind your fingers though! Shown right.

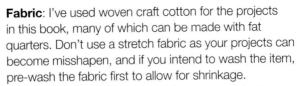

Fabric: I've used woven craft cotton for the projects in this book, many of which can be made with fat quarters. Don't use a stretch fabric as your projects can become misshapen, and if you intend to wash the item, pre-wash the fabric first to allow for shrinkage.

Thread: ideally you should use the same content as your fabric: cotton for cotton and polyester for man-made. With these projects, as they're not garments, I'd just make sure you use the best quality you can afford. The better the quality, the stronger your stitches will be.

Buttons: these are always useful, and not just for fastenings! They can be delightful embellishments, and a great disguise for wonky stitching!

Ribbon: I like to keep a few rolls of ribbon in my stash, as bows are pretty decorations and can brighten up anything from plant pots to pillowcases.

Wadding (batting): I like to use bamboo wadding (batting) as it keeps its shape well, has a lovely softness and drape, and isn't too expensive. Natural wadding (batting) like cotton or wool is nice to touch but cool wash it if you need to. For projects like the table runner (see pages 118–119) use an insulated wadding (batting) to help keep the heat away from your table or for the bottle cooler (see pages 120–123) to keep your drinks colder for longer.

Before you start

Some simple stitches

Familiarise yourself with the following stitches and, though really simple to learn, they will give your sewing project a neat, professional finish.

STRAIGHT MACHINE STITCH

This is the most used stitch for joining together your fabric, and it can also be used as a decorative topstitch and to neaten an edge.

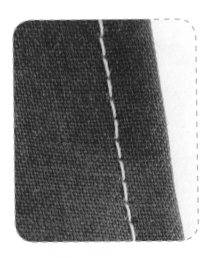

RUNNING STITCH

The most basic and most used hand stitch, this is used as a topstitch to decorate projects such as the felt gift bags (see pages 102–103). The running stitch on the rustic bunting (pages 24–25) used six strands of embroidery thread and a large-eyed needle.

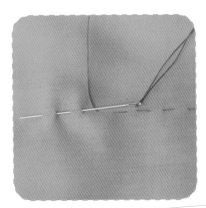

BACKSTITCH

This is a good stitch to use on stretch fabric as it 'gives' a little, and is a useful stitch to embroider lines, as on the holly leaves on pages 100 and 106. Take the needle through the fabric, then put it back through just behind where you started, and up again in front. The stitches will overlap on the back of the fabric.

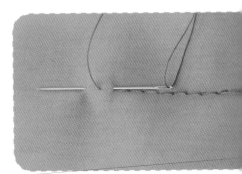

GATHERING

To gather, as with the Scandinavian gnome (see page 45), knot the end of a strong thread and make a row of running stitches about ¼in (0.5cm) long. When you've stitched the length you require, gently pull the thread to make the gathers. If you're gathering a longer length of fabric I'd recommend sewing two rows as this helps the gathers to sit flat.

You can also gather with your sewing machine: loosen the tension and use the longest stitch. At each end of the row of stitches leave a few inches of thread. Knot one end, and pull the bottom thread from the other end to gather. Don't forget to reset the tension on your machine before you carry on sewing.

LADDER STITCH

Use this hand stitch to close openings, as with my Scandinavian hanging hearts (see pages 50–53). Make the stitches as small as you can to match with the machine stitching either side. When sewn well, you shouldn't see the stitches at all! Take the needle straight across the opening, into the fold of fabric and out again, then back across the opening. Your stitches will look like the rungs of a ladder.

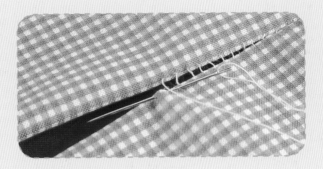

TACKING (BASTING) STITCH

This is a long hand stitch that temporarily holds the fabric together before machine sewing. Use a contrast colour thread so that it's easy to see when removing. This is really useful when fitting zips, as in my mistletoe wreath pillow cover (see pages 72–75), as trying to sew around pins can cause the zip to move.

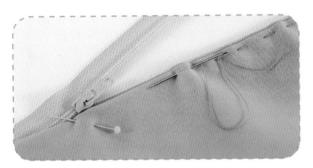

BLANKET STITCH

This stitch can help to stop fraying of woven fabrics, and is used to finish off the edges of fabrics like felt, giving a hand-made look to the project (see pages 102–103 and 104–105). Take the needle through the fabric about ¼in (0.5cm) from the edge, and loop the thread over the needle before pulling through.

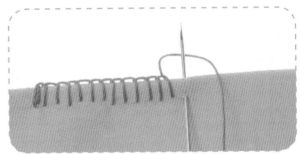

SLIP STITCH

This stitch has many names – whip stitch and blind stitch to name a couple – and is used for attaching bias tape and hemming. I've used a contrast thread here so that you can see the stitches, but use the same colour thread to make the stitches as invisible as possible. Take the needle through the fabric and catch the bias tape and hem with as small a stitch as you can. This was used for the tree skirt on pages 76–79.

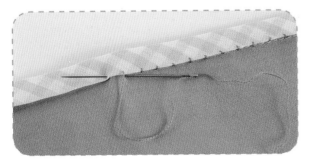

OVER-EDGE STITCH

This stitch is used decoratively, or to help stop woven fabric from fraying. I used it to close the openings on my monochrome Christmas tree (see pages 90–91) as it's a quick stitch and in this case, as the stitching was on the bottom of my work, it wouldn't be seen. Take the needle through the fabric, over the edge and back through again.

FRENCH KNOTS

You'll see these little knots grouped together to form the centre of flowers, used individually as eyes on motifs or scattered randomly on plain fabric to add interest and texture. Knot the thread at the back of your fabric and take the needle through to the front. At the point where the thread comes out of the fabric, wrap the thread around the needle a couple of times. Holding the thread to help stop it knotting too soon, gently pull the needle through, the thread will form a small knot on top of the fabric. Push the needle back through the same hole and move to the next knot.

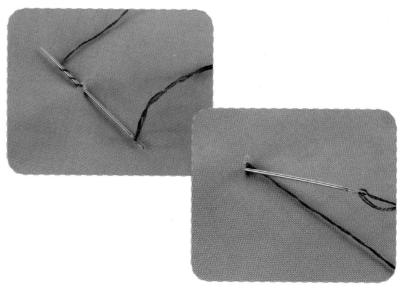

Cutting bias strips

Making your own bias tape is both economical and effective as you're not limited to the colours you find in stores. Now you can make contrasting or matching tape from any fabric you like!

1 You will need to cut strips at a 45-degree angle, so a rotary cutter and mat is essential. Cut 2in (5cm) strips to make 1in (2.5cm) bias binding.

2 To make the tape, feed through a bias tape maker and press.

Joining together bias strips

1 Place the two pieces of bias fabric right sides together at right angles to each other.

2 Sew from one corner to the other as in the photograph.

3 Trim the seam back to 1/8in (3mm) and press open. Make the tape by feeding through a bias tape maker as in step 2 above.

Applying bias tape

I use a lot of bias tape in my projects – it gives a finished, professional look to things like placemats and table runners. Sometimes I use shop-bought tape and sometimes I like to make my own. Whichever you choose, the application is the same.

1 Open up the tape and pin right sides together to the edge of your project.

2 Sew along the creased line, taking out the pins as you go.

3 When you meet the start of the tape, overlap by about ¼in (0.5cm).

4 Fold the tape over the edge to the wrong side of your work, pin to the back, then slip stitch to secure.

Mitred corners

1 Sew along the crease line as usual, but stop ¼in (0.5cm) from the end of your work and reverse a couple of stitches.

2 Pinch the corner of the tape, matching up the raw edges with the second side of fabric.

3 Start sewing at the edge of the fabric, again along the crease line.

4 Fold the tape over and you'll see a neat fold in the corner.

5 Pin the corners, then hand sew on the back when you've completed all four.

Making a square bag base

I use this technique quite a lot on bags and purses, and it works well on the bottle coolers (pages 120–123) to give a square base.

1 Firstly, when you've sewn the sides of the bag together, fold the bottom seam over the side seam and pin. Make sure the seams are lined up – you can feel the seams through the fabric.

2 Measure from the point, across the bottom seam according to the instructions for your project, and mark with a pencil.

3 Sew across this line, back-tacking at each end of the stitch line.

4 Cut away the corners of the fabric.

5 When turned, the corners should look like this.

Free-motion embroidery

I'm such a fan of this technique, and used it throughout my Contemporary Christmas chapter (see page 108). You'll need a free-motion or darning foot for your sewing machine, and the ability to drop the feed dogs. Feed dogs are the 'teeth' under your machine's needles, which feed the fabric through. When these are dropped, you have to move the fabric to create stitches. Forwards or backwards, left or right, the faster you move the fabric the longer the stitches. You're literally drawing with needle and thread, and the best thing is, you don't have to be an artist!

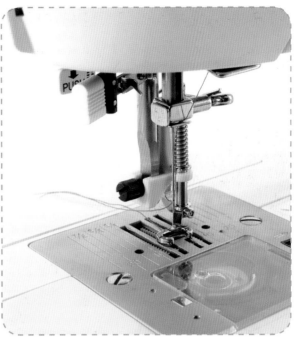

Your free-motion foot will look something like this, and you can see here that the feed teeth have been dropped.

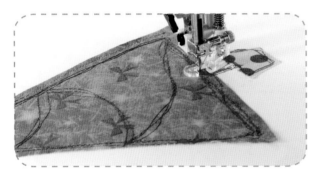

Your designs can be swirls, straight lines, waves or zigzags. There are no rules, so enjoy getting creative!

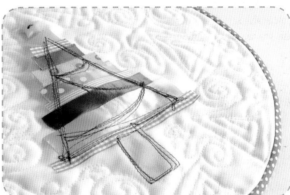

Snipping into curves

With curves, snip little 'v' shapes around the seam allowance, being careful not to cut the stitches. This reduces bulk and stops the seam from puckering.

Cutting across corners

Before turning a corner the right side out, cut the fabric across the point, close to the stitches – this will reduce the bulk and make your corner neater.

Rustic Christmas

The natural colours and textures of burlap/hessian, string and linen with a contrast of red fabric and ribbon gives a homely and inviting feel to this room. Decorated twigs add simple style, while the glow from a few candles in decorative pots creates a cosy Christmas atmosphere.

Advent Calendar

This stunning Advent calendar will decorate your home every December for years to come! Fill each pocket with sweets and candy, small toys, make-up or vouchers.

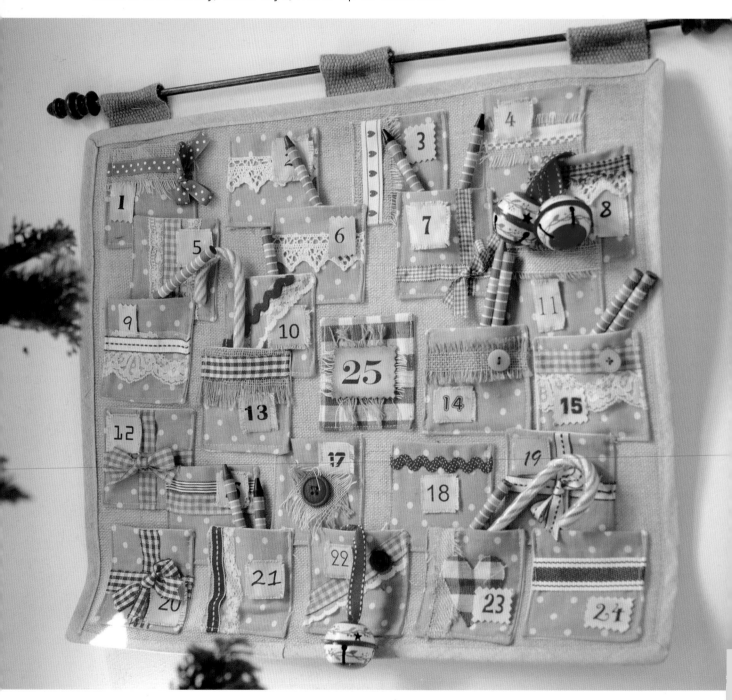

What you need

One piece of lightweight burlap/hessian measuring 18 x 20in (46 x 51cm)

One piece of stiff fusible fabric stabiliser measuring 18 x 20in (46 x 51cm)

One piece of backing fabric measuring 18 x 20in (46 x 51cm)

Twenty-four squares of linen-effect fabric measuring 3½in (9cm) square

One piece of red gingham fabric measuring 3½in (9cm) square

Twenty-five pieces of calico or similar measuring 3½in (9cm) square for the back of the pockets

One sheet of printable canvas

2 yards (1.85m) of 1in (2.5cm) bias binding

A selection of ribbon, lace, frayed medium-weight burlap/hessian and buttons to decorate

Three pieces of medium-weight burlap/hessian tape measuring 5in (13cm) each for hanging

Repositionable spray fabric adhesive

Fabric glue

Pinking shears

Pole for hanging

1 After cutting the twenty-four square pocket pieces, the first thing to do is decorate them. I sewed strips of ribbon or lace – or both – to the front of each, making each square different. Add buttons and bows as well if you wish!

2 Place each piece, including the red gingham square, right sides together with a calico square and sew around three sides, leaving the bottom edge open.

3 Snip away the excess fabric at the corners to reduce the seam bulk and turn the right way out.

21

4 Fold the raw edges inwards and press into place.

5 To create the numbers for the pockets, I printed 1–25 onto printable canvas, using different fonts available on my PC. Make the number '25' larger than the rest.

6 Press with a hot iron to make the ink permanent.

7 Cut out each number, and fray or trim the edges with pinking shears.

8 To give the numbers an aged look, paint them with diluted black tea or coffee, or use distress inks.

9 To make the number '25' stand out, shade the edges with an ink pad. Fray a square of burlap/hessian and sit this behind the number.

10 Fuse the stabiliser to the back of the lightweight burlap/hessian with your iron.

11 Arrange the pockets on the lightweight burlap/hessian. Placing them randomly and overlapping them slightly disguises any pockets that aren't perfectly square, but don't overlap them so much that you won't be able to put a gift inside! I've placed the number twenty-five right in the centre, with no pockets overlapping it.

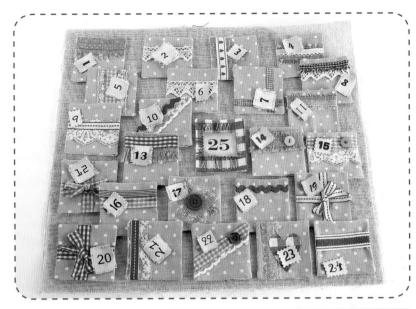

12 When you're happy with the arrangement, pin each pocket in place then carefully sew around three sides, leaving the top of each pocket open. Reverse a couple of stitches at the start and end of your stitches to strengthen the top of the pockets. Start with the top pockets and work your way carefully downwards. Glue the numbers in place on their pockets.

13 Using the repositionable spray adhesive, place the calendar on top of the backing fabric.

14 Sew the bias tape all the way round (see page 15). Although, as the back of the calendar is unlikely to be seen, you could glue the bias binding to the back of the calendar instead of hand sewing it.

15 Fold the lengths of burlap/hessian tape in half and pin them, evenly spaced, across the back of the calendar. Sew them in place.

16 Thread a pole through your burlap/hessian loops and fill all the pockets with presents!

Tip
It is best to cut your backing fabric too large then trim it to size, to make sure there's enough room to arrange your pockets.

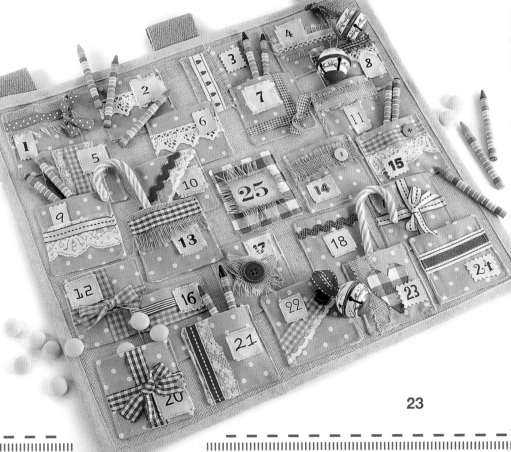

Bunting

So very simple! No hemming or even straight sewing is required, and the more fraying the better, as this creates an effective rustic decoration.

What you need

For 72in (183cm) of bunting you will need:

3 yards (2.8m) of ¼in (0.5cm) rope (including extra length for tying)

½ yard (46cm) of medium-weight burlap/hessian

A 5in (13cm) strip of red gingham fabric

Scraps of lightweight burlap/hessian or linen to cut into hearts

A few small pieces of ribbon for bows

Strong fabric glue

Red embroidery thread and large-eyed needle

1 Cut the medium-weight burlap/hessian into nine triangles, each measuring 5in (13cm) across the top and 9in (23cm) long.

2 Cut the gingham fabric into nine triangles, each measuring 4in (10cm) across the top and 5in (13cm) long.

3 Pull the edges of both fabrics to fray them a little.

4 Hand sew a simple running stitch along the two longer sides of each burlap/hessian triangle with the embroidery thread. These stitches don't have to be neat or even.

5 Lay each gingham triangle on top of each burlap/hessian pennant and secure with a few spots of glue along the top edge.

6 Lay the pennants out so that they are about 3in (7.5cm) apart, then glue the rope across the top.

7 Add a few hearts and bows to finish; secure them with glue or a few stitches.

Tip

If you enjoy hand sewing, you could add decorative stitches, such as cross stitching, to the bunting.

Candle Pots

Although there's no sewing with these candle holders, they are such fun to make and cost very little. I'd suggest if you're burning real candles you don't paint the inside of the pots, so that the heat doesn't bubble the paint.

1 In a well-ventilated area, spray paint both the outside and inside of the plant pot, and leave to dry.

2 Put a strip of double-sided tape around the middle of the pot and peel off the backing.

3 Fray the edges of your burlap/hessian strip, making a fringe of about ¼in (0.5cm).

5 Wrap the lace around the pot, on top of the burlap/hessian, then wrap the string on top of this, tying it in a bow.

4 Wrap the length of frayed burlap/hessian around the pot.

Tip
If you don't want to burn real candles, try battery-operated tea lights instead.

Present Sack

How exciting to find these sacks filled with gifts on Christmas morning! The raw-edge appliqué will fray slightly, which adds to the look of this rustic Christmas item.

What you need

Two pieces of lightweight burlap/hessian measuring 12 x 16in (30.5 x 41cm)

Two pieces of lining fabric measuring 12 x 18in (30.5 x 46cm)

Four squares of fabric for the appliqué, each measuring 4in (10cm) square

A 30in (76cm) length of string to tie

Tape to thread the string through, 24in (61cm) long

Tape ribbon to decorate, 30in (76cm) long – you will cut this into two strips of 8in (20.5cm) and tie a bow with the rest

Repositionable spray adhesive

A large safety pin

1 Cut and prepare all your fabrics before you begin.

2 Place the four squares together on the front of the sack; position them centrally, about 4in (10cm) from the bottom of the bag, and fix in place with the spray adhesive.

3 Sew around the edges of each square.

4 Add the tape ribbon strips on top, sew in place, then hand sew the bow to the top of the 'present'.

5 Place a piece of lining fabric on top of the front of the sack, with the right sides facing, and the top edges aligned. Sew along this top edge Repeat this process to join the second piece of lining fabric to the piece that will form the back of the sack.

6 Open out the pieces and place them right sides together. Sew all the way around, leaving a gap of about 3in (7.5cm) in the base of the lining for turning.

7 Turn the right way out, and hand sew the opening closed using ladder stitch.

8 Push the lining inside the sack. As the lining fabric is 2in (5cm) longer overall, it will fold over to give a contrasting trim around the top of the sack; press.

9 Pin the tape around the top of the sack, 2in (5cm) from the top edge. Leave a gap in the centre front to allow the string to pass through.

10 Sew along each side of the tape, back-tacking at the start and end of each row to strengthen the stitches; leave the ends unsewn. You may need to use the free arm on your sewing machine for this.

11 Knot the end of the string and attach to the safety pin, then thread through the tape. Your sack is now ready to fill with gifts.

Tip
Make a set of matching gift tags from rectangles of corrugated cardboard with the corners snipped off, and glue a frayed square of lightweight burlap/hessian and a heart to the front.

String Baubles

This no-sew project is quick to make and the final result is lightweight and ideal for any tree. Be careful if you have cats, as mine were very interested in scratching these!

What you need

Polystyrene balls in various sizes

A large ball of string

Ribbon, lace and paper flowers to decorate

Polystyrene glue

A few long pins

1 Cover the top half of each ball with a drizzle of glue.

2 Pin the end of the string to the top of the ball, and start to wind the string around, being careful not to let any of the polystyrene show through.

3 You may find it easier to let it dry in stages, pinning it as you go.

4 Continue gluing and winding the string until you reach the bottom, then leave the whole piece to dry completely.

5 Remove the pins, and glue a loop of string to the top to hang.

6 Glue a little bow to the top of the bauble, and a strip of lace and ribbon around the middle.

7 Add flowers, beads, string or anything else that takes your fancy!

Tip

Try this method with different shapes of polystyrene moulds: this cone makes a delightful little Christmas tree, decorated with bakers' twine, ribbon and glass-headed pins! Be careful with those pins if they're in easy reach of young children…

Wreath

The charm of this wreath is its simplicity, and the contrast of textures between the medium-weight burlap/hessian and other fabrics. The little presents could be filled with cinnamon for a warming Christmassy fragrance.

What you need

For the wreath

A metal wreath ring: mine measures 14in (35.5cm) across, bought from my local florist

36in (91cm) of florists' wire

½ yard (46cm) of medium-weight burlap/hessian, cut into four strips of 4½in (11.5cm)

For the presents

Four squares of red fabric measuring 4in (10cm)

Four squares of cream fabric measuring 4in (10cm)

Two squares of red fabric measuring 3in (7.5cm)

Four squares of striped fabric measuring 3in (7.5cm), or you could use any scrap fabrics you already have

48in (122cm) of gingham ribbon

36in (91cm) of red ribbon

24in (61cm) of white ribbon

12in (30.5cm) of beige ribbon

36in (91cm) of bakers' twine, to attach parcels

Toy stuffing

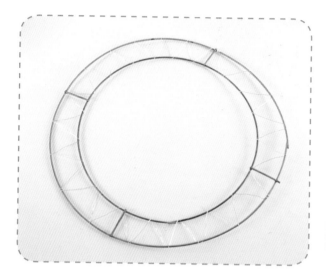

1 The gaps in my wreath ring were too wide, so I wrapped the florists' wire around the ring to make small openings to hold my fabric.

2 Take a strip of medium-weight burlap/hessian, and push it through the gaps in the wreath without going all the way through to create this 'puffy' effect. The rough texture will hold it in place.

3 Don't worry about sewing the strips together – just make sure that the ends of the burlap/hessian strips are to the back of the wreath.

4 Starting at the back of the wreath, wrap the gingham ribbon all the way around, and knot at the back when finished.

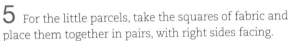

5 For the little parcels, take the squares of fabric and place them together in pairs, with right sides facing.

6 Sew around the edge of each set of squares, back-tacking at the start and end of your stitching, and leaving a gap of about 1½in (4cm) in one side for turning. Snip away the excess fabric at the corners.

7 Turn each of your squares the right way out.

8 Stuff each with the toy stuffing, then sew across the opening with an overhand stitch.

9 Wrap the ribbon around the parcels and tie in a bow: you might want to put a couple of the smaller parcels on top of a larger one before tying.

10 Using the bakers' twine, tie the parcels evenly around the wreath.

Tip

Make your wreath a little different by adding pine cones and greenery, then a large burlap/hessian bow!

Tip

To create a pile of presents as a decoration to go elsewhere in your home, try this: I used two squares of fabric measuring 4½in (11.5cm), two measuring 3½in (9cm) and two measuring 2½in (6.5cm) made up in the same way as the wreath parcels then tied all together with ribbon. This would also make a cute pincushion!

Scandinavian Christmas

Rustic, refined, warm and cheerful, all rolled into one! The splash of red in my Scandinavian Christmas décor creates impact, the elongated heart, cones and stocking add festive elegance, and the gnomes provide a touch of humour. Coffee and cinnamon cake, anyone?

Christmas Cones

These fabric cones are a fun way to decorate your tree: fill them with sweets, little homemade cookies or festively fragranced cinnamon sticks.

What you need

Two circles of contrasting fabric measuring 8in (20.5cm) across

Four lengths of ¼in (0.5cm) wide ribbon, each 10in (25.5cm) long

Eight small buttons

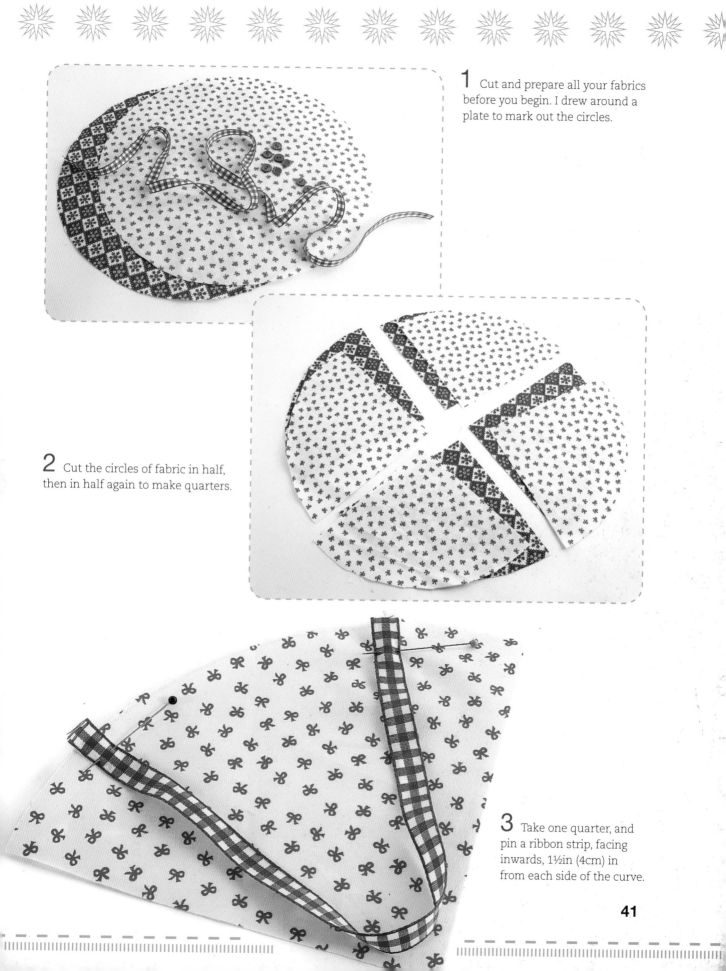

1 Cut and prepare all your fabrics before you begin. I drew around a plate to mark out the circles.

2 Cut the circles of fabric in half, then in half again to make quarters.

3 Take one quarter, and pin a ribbon strip, facing inwards, 1½in (4cm) in from each side of the curve.

4 Tack the ribbon ends in place and remove the pins.

5 Place a contrasting piece of fabric over the top, right sides together, pin in place, and sew across the curved edge.

6 Open out your joined piece of fabric and refold it, with the right sides facing inwards, to create an elongated diamond shape. Pin the straight sides together then sew along them, leaving a gap of 2in (5cm) on whichever piece of fabric will sit on the inside of your cone.

7 Trim the seam allowances at the points. Turn the right way out and stitch the gap in the lining closed.

8 Push the lining of the cone inside the outer fabric.

9 Carefully press around the top of the cone, to leave a small band of the lining showing. Then add a button at each end of the hanging ribbon for decoration.

Tip
If your fabric is a little too lightweight to hold its shape, use spray starch to add stability.

43

Christmas Gnomes

One of the many Scandinavian customs at Christmas time is to leave a bowl of porridge out for these little fellows, to persuade them to leave gifts under the tree for well-behaved children! Please bear in mind that this little gnome is an ornament, and isn't suitable as a toy.

What you need

A circle of fabric for the base measuring 8in (20.5cm) across – I drew around a plate

For the body, two pieces of the same fabric measuring 5in (13cm) wide by 6in (15.5cm) long

For the hat, a rectangle of contrasting fabric measuring 7 x 9in (18 x 23cm)

A curtain weight for the base

A bead for the nose

44in (112cm) of ¼in (0.5cm) cording for the hair

12in (30.5cm) of ribbon, ¼in (0.5cm) wide

A couple of handfuls of wadding (batting) to stuff

Needle and thread

Fabric glue

1 Knot the end of the thread and sew a running stitch around the edge of your fabric circle, about ¼in (0.5cm) from the edge. When you've sewn all the way round, gently pull the thread to start gathering.

2 Before gathering completely, pop the weight into the bottom of the circle, then stuff with wadding (batting). Draw up the gathering thread completely and sew over a few stitches to secure it. This is the base.

3 Cut two triangles from the body fabric, measuring 5in (13cm) across the bottom and 6in (15.5cm) tall.

45

4 Place one triangle on top of the other, right sides together. Sew together along the two long edges. Snip off the seam allowance at the point.

5 Turn the cone the right way out – this will form the body of your gnome. Push some stuffing inside it to give it some shape.

6 Push the round base piece created in step 1 into the bottom of your gnome's body; tuck the raw edges of the body piece under.

7 Hand sew the two pieces together all the way round the bottom of the body. It doesn't matter how neat your stitches are as they'll be covered with ribbon.

8 Glue the wrong side of your ribbon and secure it in place on top of this seam.

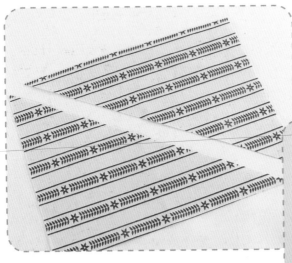

9 To create the hat, take your rectangle of fabric and cut it diagonally in two.

10 Fold over the two long sides of one triangle, right sides facing, to make a cone shape, and sew along the joined edge.

46

11 Turn the cone the right way out, and trim across the bottom to make it straight.

12 Put a little stuffing inside – you'll see the cone shape starting to twist because of the way it's been cut.

13 Fold under the raw edge and press.

14 Cut the cord into 2in (5cm) lengths.

15 Apply a small amount of glue to one side at the end of the pieces, and stick them vertically all the way around the body, about 1in (2.5cm) from the top.

16 When they have dried, pop a little more glue over the top of them and place the hat on top. Fray the ends of the cords slightly to look like hair.

17 Glue or sew on the bead for the nose.

Tip
Many a well-dressed gnome would have a bell or a tassel on his hat, and buttons on his tunic!

47

Scrap Fabric Wreath

What a great way to use up your scraps of fabric: it's quick, easy and there's no sewing involved!

What you need

A polystyrene ring

Scraps of fabric cut into pieces approximately 1½in (4cm) square

Glue that is suitable to use with polystyrene

A blunt pencil

A piece of cord measuring about 6in (15.5cm) long

About 20in (51cm) of red gingham ribbon for a bow

1 Prepare all your squares of fabric. These don't have to be exact, and don't worry about them fraying – that adds to the look!

2 Pop a blob of glue onto the wrong side of a few squares of your fabric.

3 Place one piece glue-side down onto the ring, and push into the polystyrene using the blunt pencil.

4 Repeat this process until the whole ring is covered.

5 When dry, turn over the wreath and attach the cord to hang in the same way.

6 Create a bow using your gingham ribbon, and secure to the bottom centre of the wreath with glue.

Tip
Don't stop at a wreath – you could also buy polystyrene cones and make matching scrap Christmas trees.

Hanging Heart

I've made these hearts longer than usual as I think it adds to the Scandinavian look. I've filled them with toy stuffing but you could add fragrance to the filling if you wish.

1 To make the template, draw a centre line along your card.

2 Place the lid to the right of the line, so that it slightly overlaps it. Draw around it.

3 Join the side of the circle to the centre line, 4½in (11.5cm) below the bottom of the circle.

4 Fold the heart in half along the centre line, and cut it out. When you open it up again you'll have a perfect heart shape.

5 Take the rectangle of fabric that will form the back of the heart, and cut it in half lengthways.

6 Then sew it back together with a ¼in (0.5cm) seam allowance. Press the seam open.

7 Lay the heart template centrally over the seam. Draw around it then cut out your heart shape.

8 Cut out another fabric heart shape using your template. This will form the front of the heart – you don't need to create a seam in this piece.

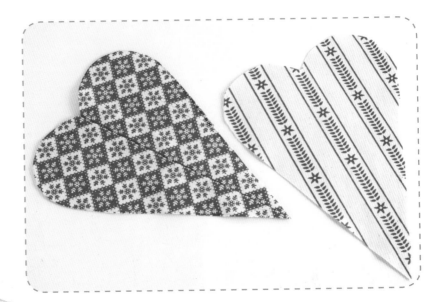

9 Sew the two hearts right sides together all the way around.

10 Take your quick unpick and make a hole in the back seam. Turn your heart the right way through and poke out the point.

11 Stuff the heart tightly with toy stuffing.

12 Sew the opening closed with ladder stitch.

13 Hand sew the ribbon loop for hanging to the front, adding a button to the centre.

Tip

Make each heart slightly different by mixing up your fabric, bows and buttons, or use bakers' twine as a hanging loop.

Christmas Stocking

To keep with the Scandinavian decorative feel, this Christmas stocking is long and thin, but wide enough to hold a few gifts! It's fully lined and could be padded if you wish, to give a more luxurious feel.

1 Take the card, ruler and pencil and draw two rectangles, one measuring 14 x 6in (35.5 x 15.5cm) and one measuring 8 x 6in (20.5 x 15.5cm). Cut them out.

2 Mark 1in (2.5cm) in from each long edge at the base of the longer rectangle, and draw a line from these marks to the top corners; this will taper the leg shape. Cut along these lines.

3 On the smaller rectangle, draw a diagonal line from one corner to the top, about 2in (5cm) from the opposite corner. Don't worry about these measurements being exact – these stockings aren't to be worn!

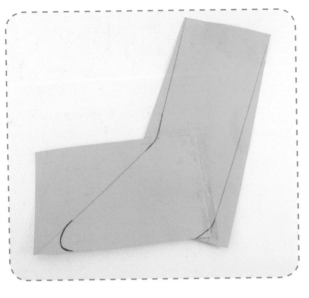

4 Place the smaller rectangle of card over the bottom of the long one, and turn it about 30-degrees or until it looks like a foot. Secure with sticky tape.

5 Round off the toe and heel.

6 Cut out the stocking shape.

7 Fold the outer fabric in half right sides together and draw around the stocking template.

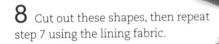

8 Cut out these shapes, then repeat step 7 using the lining fabric.

9 Before sewing together, it's time to decorate the front of the stocking. As stockings are usually hung against a wall or fireplace, there's little point in decorating the back…

10 Trim your strips of ribbon to slightly different lengths and line up the ends about 2in (5cm) from the top of the stocking.

11 Sew the ribbon ends in place. You could actually glue the ribbon ends if you prefer, as these stockings don't usually go in the wash!

12 Sew the pompom trim over the ends of the ribbons to tidy.

13 Sew another strip of ribbon across the top.

14 Add a little pompom to the end of each strip of ribbon.

15 Place one of the lining pieces right side down on top of your decorated stocking front. Sew along the seam at the top. Repeat for the back of the stocking with the second piece of lining. Open both shapes out.

16 Make a loop from ribbon for hanging, and tack it in line with the sewn ribbon on the front of the stocking, facing inwards.

17 Pin your opened-out stocking pieces right sides together, then sew all the way round taking a ¼in (0.5cm) seam allowance, and leaving a gap of about 3in (7.5cm) at the bottom of the lining for turning. Make sure the tassels are tucked in so you don't sew them into the seam!

18 Turn the right way out, and hand stitch the opening closed.

19 Push the lining into the outer stocking.

20 Finally add the large pompom to the top of the toe.

Tip
Try putting bells onto the ribbon instead of pompoms – that would create a lovely Christmassy jingle!

Traditional Christmas

Deck your halls in the traditional Christmas colours of evergreen, snow white and heart red; a touch of gold adds the magic. This room takes me back to my childhood Christmases, sneaking downstairs at a ridiculously early hour to see if the Christmas stockings were bulging with gifts, and to see if Santa Claus had eaten the mince pie we had left him in the fireplace. Not forgetting Rudolph the red-nosed reindeer, who was partial to a carrot or two!

Ball Decorations

This project is not as complicated as it might look! And it is a great way to use up small pieces of left-over fabric. These little balls would make fun toys for youngsters or unusual decorations for Christmas.

What you need

Six 8in (20.5cm) circles of cotton fabric, any pattern or plain

A 5in (13cm) strip of ribbon for hanging, plus extra to create a bow

Kapok filling to stuff

Pinking shears (optional)

Needle and thread

1 Draw around a small plate or similar and cut six circular pieces of fabric.

2 Pair the circles up and place each set right sides together. Straight stitch around the edge of each of the circles, with a ¼in (0.5cm) seam allowance, leaving a gap of 2in (5cm) for turning and stuffing, as shown.

3 Trim around the edge of your shape with pinking shears, making sure you don't cut through your stitches – this will make the seam neater when you turn the circle through. Alternatively cut little 'V' shapes into the edge, right the way around.

4 Turn each circle the right way out.

5 Lay all three layers on top of each other, lining up the turning gaps so they are all in the same place.

6 Fold the circles in half and crease with your fingers.

7 Slide a loop of ribbon in between the top of two layers – make sure about ½in (1cm) is tucked inside.

8 Sew up the crease and across the centre only of the turning gaps, joining all three circles together and trapping the loop of ribbon in place.

9 Stuff your wadding through the six gaps. Use a pencil or similar to ensure the stuffing reaches right to the top of each semi-circle.

10 Hand stitch the six turning gaps closed – use a ladder stitch and a complementary thread colour.

11 Hand sew the ribbon loop in place to ensure that it is secure. If this is a toy for a child, please make sure your stitches are really secure so that the ribbon doesn't come loose.

12 Create and sew on a little bow as decoration.

Tips

Add a trimming to the stitched edges for a more decorative effect.

A string of beads dangling from the bottom of the ball decoration adds extra interest.

Make the circles large or small: I'm thinking dinner plates or saucers!

A string of ball decorations would make a pretty swag.

Stocking Decorations

These little Christmas bootees could decorate a tree or a fireplace, and could be filled with chocolate coins as a surprise Christmas treat!

What you need

For each stocking you will need approximately 6 x 10in (15.5 x 25.5cm) of patterned fabric and 6 x 10in (15.5 x 25.5cm) of plain lining fabric
Ribbon, buttons, ric-rac edging and bows, to decorate as you wish
6in (15.5cm) of ribbon for each stocking for a hanging loop
Pinking shears

1 The template for the stocking is given on page 128. To create your shapes, fold your patterned fabric in half, wrong sides together, and cut out a pair of stocking shapes. Repeat this for the lining fabric. Pair together two patterned and two plain stocking shapes.

2 Sew the top of each patterned piece to the top of a lining piece, right sides together.

3 Open out these sewn stocking pieces and place the two of them right sides together. Sew all the way round, leaving a gap in the bottom of the lining for turning.

4 Trim the edge with pinking shears – this will help to keep the seams neat when turned.

5 Turn the right way out and sew the opening closed.

6 Push the lining down inside the bootee.

7 Fold over the top to show off the lining.

8 Add a little bow or other trimmings to your mini stocking. As it's unlikely these stockings will ever be washed, there's nothing wrong with using glue to add your trims!

Tip

Make 25 little stockings and number them. Attach them to a length of ribbon to create a cute hanging Advent calendar!

9 Repeat to create further stockings and decorate them as you wish. Sew the ribbon loops to the back of each stocking and hang on the tree!

Christmas Stocking

Christmas stockings nowadays can be glitzy and glamorous, patchwork and quilted or shabby and chic, but this stocking is simply traditional. The only decoration is the jumbo ric-rac around the top, but feel free to embellish as you like! The simplest way to make a pattern is to draw around a sock – this gives the basic shape for the stocking, then you can make it as big as you like!

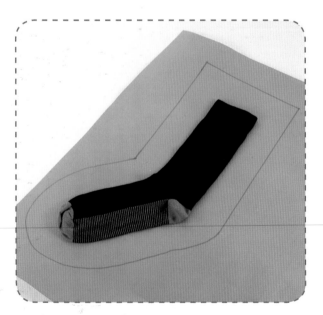

1 Draw around the sock, adding a 2in (5cm) border all the way round. You may need to extend the top – my stocking measures 17in (43cm) tall.

2 Using the template, cut out two pieces from the wadding (batting) and two pieces from the lining. Place your two pieces of outer fabric right sides together and then use the template to cut through both layers – this will ensure that you cut a 'front' and a 'back' piece.

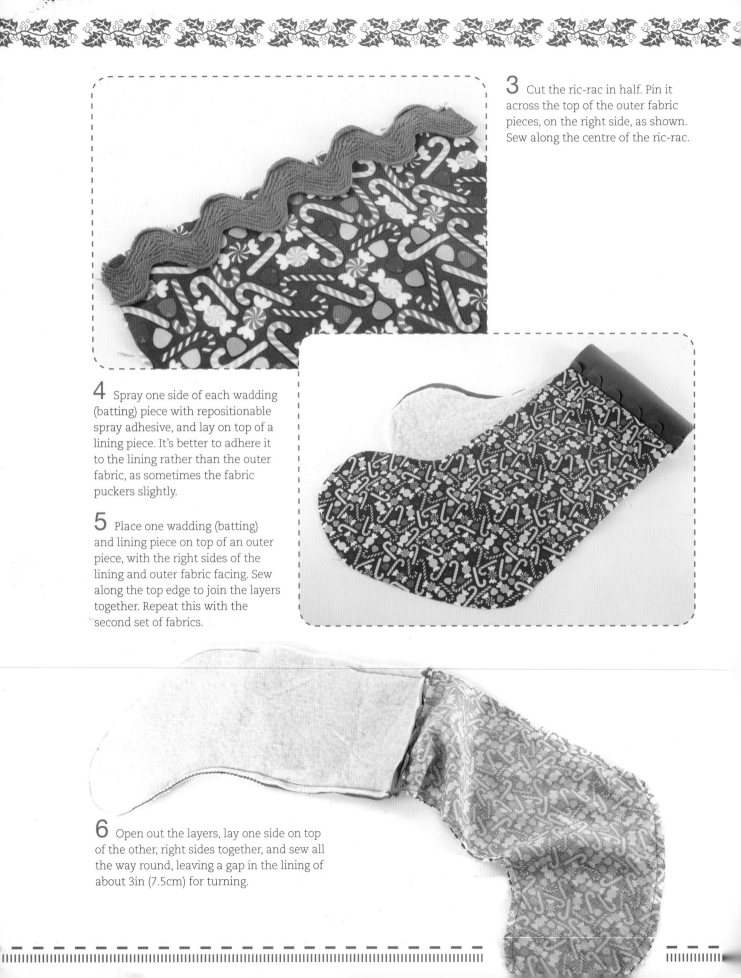

3 Cut the ric-rac in half. Pin it across the top of the outer fabric pieces, on the right side, as shown. Sew along the centre of the ric-rac.

4 Spray one side of each wadding (batting) piece with repositionable spray adhesive, and lay on top of a lining piece. It's better to adhere it to the lining rather than the outer fabric, as sometimes the fabric puckers slightly.

5 Place one wadding (batting) and lining piece on top of an outer piece, with the right sides of the lining and outer fabric facing. Sew along the top edge to join the layers together. Repeat this with the second set of fabrics.

6 Open out the layers, lay one side on top of the other, right sides together, and sew all the way round, leaving a gap in the lining of about 3in (7.5cm) for turning.

7 Snip into the seam allowance around the curves. You could use pinking shears if you have them.

8 Turn the stocking right side out and press.

9 Hand sew the gap in the lining closed, then push the lining inside the stocking.

10 Hand sew a loop of ribbon to the back of the stocking and hide the stitches with a button.

Tip

If you take off the ribbon loop this stocking is actually reversible: use a different pattern on the inside and your youngsters will think they have a new stocking next year!

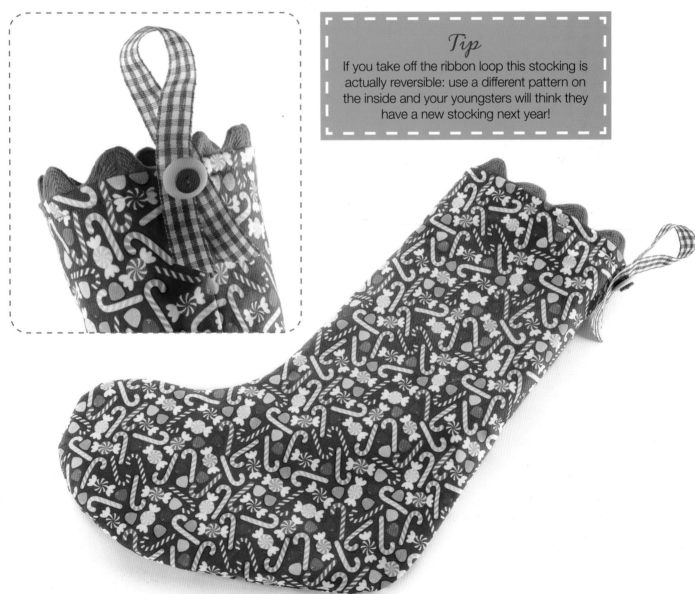

Festive Gift Bag

Fill this bag with Christmas treats and make a pretty presentation for your festive gift, then re-use as a doorstop by popping in a bag of rice!

What you need

A circle of outer fabric measuring 8in (20.5cm) across

A circle of lining fabric measuring 8in (20.5cm) across

A piece of outer fabric measuring 12 x 25in (30.5 x 63.5cm)

Lining fabric measuring 12 x 25in (30.5 x 63.5cm)

24in (61cm) ribbon: mine has wired edges

Needle and thread

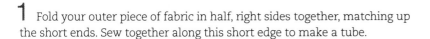

1 Fold your outer piece of fabric in half, right sides together, matching up the short ends. Sew together along this short edge to make a tube.

2 Pin the circular piece of outer fabric to one end of your tube, aligning the raw edges of both pieces, then sew together.

3 Repeat steps 1 and 2 with the lining fabric, but this time leave a gap of about 3in (7.5cm) around the rim of the base for turning.

4 Place the main bag inside the lining, right sides together, match the top seam and stitch it. Turn the right way out.

5 Sew the turning hole closed with ladder stitch.

6 Push the lining inside the outer fabric; press. Fill with goodies then tie the ribbon into a bow around the top of the bag.

Tip

Here's how to make the bag in different sizes. Measure the diameter of the circular base then take away a ¼in (0.5cm) seam allowance. Multiply this measurement by pi (3.142) then add ½in (1cm) – two seam allowances. Round the measurement up to the nearest ¼in (0.5cm) and you have the length of the fabric.

Mistletoe Wreath Pillow Cover

This red and green plaid pillow topped with a wreath of felt leaves makes a wonderful Christmas statement, and although the piping is quite time-consuming and takes a lot of fabric, it's worth it for this rich finishing touch. My pillow pad measures 18in (46cm) square but you could reduce the sizes for a smaller pillow. I like my pillows to be well-filled and plump, so I cut my fabric to the same size as the pad, which means that after sewing, the cover is slightly smaller than the pad.

What you need

18in (46cm) square pillow pad

One piece of plaid fabric, 18 x 18in (46 x 46cm)

Two rectangles for the back, each measuring 18 x 10in (46 x 25.5cm)

One 14in (36cm) nylon zip: I use continuous zip so that I can cut the length I require

75in (190.5cm) of ½in (1cm) wide piping

7¾ yards (7.1m) of 2½in (6.5cm) wide bias-cut fabric: you'll have to join a few strips together

Light green felt

Dark green felt

A handful of white plastic beads

Tailors' chalk

A 12in (30.5cm) plate for a template

Quick unpick tool

1 Firstly cut out the felt leaves using the template given on page 128. I cut forty-five light green leaves and eighteen dark green.

2 Using tailors' chalk, draw around the plate centrally on the right side of the plaid fabric square.

3 Arrange the light green leaves around the circle as shown, and stitch down the middle of each leaf. You could do this either by machine or by hand.

4 Sew on the dark green leaves in the same way.

5 Fold the bias strip of fabric around the cord, and sew across the end to stop the cord from being pulled through. Gradually feed the cord and fabric through your machine, enclosing the cord, sewing about ¼in (0.5cm) from the edge of the fabric. I'm using the standard foot on my sewing machine as I don't want to get too close to the cord. As you come to the end of the cord you'll need to push the fabric so that it ruches.

6 Before applying, fold under the fabric at the open end of the cord, and pull over the end of the cord slightly. When you've sewn it to the fabric, the other end will slip inside here for a neat finish.

7 Align the raw edge of the piping with the raw edge of the plaid fabric and pin in place, all the way round your pillow. Put the zip foot on your sewing machine and sew all the way around, ¼in (0.5cm) from the edge. Be careful of the fabric trying to gather as you sew. When you get back to within a few inches of where you started, stop sewing.

8 Trim away the extra length of cord and fabric, and pop the end of the piping inside the tube where you started to sew. Hand stitch the two ends of the fabric in place.

9 Sew on the white beads for berries amongst your felt leaves – see the photograph on the facing page for reference.

10 For the back of the pillow cover, sew the long sides of the two rectangles together with a 1in (2.5cm) seam allowance. Press the seam open.

11 Lay the zip face down over the seam, pin in place, then tack all the way around. I've hand sewn the open end of the zip together to hold it in place.

12 Machine sew all the way around the zip.

13 Turn over and, using your quick unpick, carefully undo the stitches over the teeth of the zip and remove the tacking stitches.

14 Pin then sew the back of the pillow cover right sides together with the front, again using your zip foot. Leave the zip open slightly or you'll have a problem turning it the right side out! You'll be sewing through quite a few layers of fabric here, so you may have to help it through your machine.

15 Turn the pillow cover right side out and press if you need to.

16 Fold the pillow pad in half and stuff inside, pushing the filling right into the corners.

Tip
Hollow-fibre filling is fine, but feather adds weight to the pillow and will give it a luxurious feel.

Tree Skirt

The bases of Christmas trees are never the prettiest, so this simple tree skirt is the ideal solution to disguise stands and pots.

What you need

A triangle from card to use as a template, measuring 12in (30.5cm) tall and 6in (15.5cm) across the bottom. You will use this to cut sixteen triangles of fabric: I used three designs of fabric but you could choose two patterns, or keep it plain with one fabric

A circle of lining fabric measuring 24in (61cm) across. If you don't have a piece of fabric this large you could cut another sixteen triangles of lining fabric and create the shape following steps 6 and 7

A circle of wadding (batting) measuring 24in (61cm) across

2¾ yards (254cm) of 1in (2.5cm) bias tape – you will have a little left over

Repositionable spray adhesive

Three elastic hair bungees for the button loops

Three buttons

Red felt

Green felt

Hot-glue gun

Dark red and dark green marker pens

Nine beads, one for the centre of each flower

1 Cut out the felt leaf shapes: using the templates on page 128 I cut forty-five large red leaves, forty-five small red leaves and twenty-seven large green leaves. Now cut nine 1in (2.5cm) red circles. Shade one side of each leaf with the marker pens. This makes the shapes look more three-dimensional.

2 Glue the five large petals to the felt circle.

3 Glue the five small petals in the gaps.

4 Glue the leaves behind, then the bead in the centre.

5 Repeat another eight times!

6 Cut 1in (2.5cm) from the top of your triangle template, then use the template to cut sixteen fabric triangles.

7 Place two of the triangles right sides together and sew together along one long edge. Continue to add triangles in the same way until all the pieces are joined together to make an incomplete circle; press.

8 Spray the back of your incomplete circle shape with repositionable adhesive and place the wadding (batting) circle on top. Spray the lining circle and place on top of the wadding (batting). Make sure the fabrics are smooth with no wrinkles.

9 Cut around the incomplete circle shape.

10 Pin the three elastic bungees, evenly spaced, to one side of the opening.

11 Pin the bias tape all the way around the hem, trapping the elastic loops as you go. Sew in place.

12 Fold the bias tape over to the back of the piece and hand sew in position.

13 Each of your elastic pieces needs to align with a button on the other side of the opening. Mark where the buttons should sit, and sew them on.

14 Glue the poinsettias evenly around the hem.

Tip
I used my hot-glue gun to make and apply the flowers, but hand sew them if you intend to wash the skirt at any time.

Monochrome Christmas

Using just two colours creates home décor with real impact, and I think black and white with the occasional touch of red and silver is really effective for these stylish decorations. A classy Christmas indeed! Of course, if Christmas isn't the same for you without a pop of colour, try purple for drama, lilac for prettiness or icy blue hues.

Gift Box

Presentation is important, particularly when giving a hand-made gift, and this elegant box is almost a gift in itself! Fill with jewellery, cookies, sweets or pot pourri, and just see the delight on the face of the person you're giving it to...

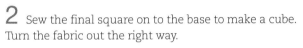

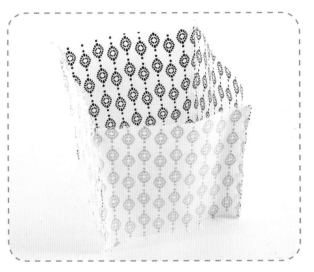

1 Iron the interfacing on to the outer panel pieces. Sew four of the squares together to make a tube.

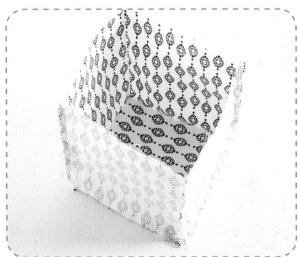

2 Sew the final square on to the base to make a cube. Turn the fabric out the right way.

3 Repeat with the lining squares, but leave one side of the base unstitched for turning. Do not turn this cube through.

4 Take the eight rectangular pieces, place the saucer over the top and draw round the curve. Cut around the drawn shape to create eight curved pieces.

5 Pair two of the curved shapes, right sides together, and sew around the curved edge. Repeat to create three other shapes.

6 Snip into the curve of each curved shape, or trim with pinking shears.

7 Turn the four curved shapes through, then press.

8 Sew the bottom straight edge of each curved piece to the top of the outer cube.

9 Drop the whole of this cube inside the lining – remember that the lining cube should be inside out.

10 Sew all the way around the top, joining the two cubes together. You may need to use the free arm of your sewing machine to do this.

11 Turn the right way out, through the unstitched section of the lining.

12 Sew the opening closed by hand, then push the lining inside the outer cube; press.

13 Cut the ribbon in half.

14 Pop a dot of fabric glue in the centre of the base of the cube, lay the middle of one piece of ribbon across the glue and, when dry, pop another dot of glue in the middle of this ribbon and lay the second ribbon on top.

15 When the glue has dried, run each of the four pieces of ribbon up the side of the cube, and glue at the top, just before you reach the curved flaps.

16 Attach the lace strip all the way around the top of the cube with more fabric glue.

17 Sew the smaller button on top of the larger one, and stitch to the front of the box to trim.

18 When you fold over the flaps and tie the bow, you'll have a beautiful little gift box!

Tip

Decorate your gift box with silk flowers or embroider on initials to make it more personal.

Fabric Baubles

With just a few fabric squares you can create these elegant baubles: plain or printed fabrics would work well, and you could add glitter, gems or tassels if you want to make them stand out!

What you need

For each bauble:

Ten pieces of fabric measuring 4in (10cm) square: I used two contrasting patterns

6in (15.5cm) length of cord for hanging

One tassel

Tip

Instead of tassels, why not string a few beads together and sew them to your bauble! Or try different sizes of squares to make an interesting display.

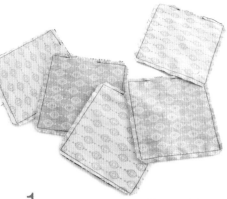

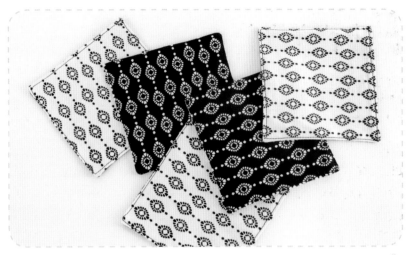

1 Sew two squares of fabric right sides together, all around the edge but leaving a gap of about 1½in (4cm) in one side for turning. Repeat four more times.

2 Snip the excess seam allowance away at the corners.

3 Turn right side out and press.

4 Topstitch all the way around each square, sewing as close to the edge as you can. Don't worry about sewing the turning gap closed as the topstitching will achieve this.

5 Lay your five squares on top of each other. Fold your length of cord in half and insert it between the layers at one point.

6 Draw a straight line from corner to corner, if you wish, then sew a straight line along it through all five layers, trapping the cord as you sew. Remember to back tack at each end to stop the stitches from coming undone. Go slowly at each end – there's quite a lot of fabric to sew through here!

7 Lift up the points of the two top triangles. With a needle and thread, hand sew together at the point. Overstitch a few times then knot, in the same spot. Repeat this to join together the remaining eight triangles, to create five joined, open-sided triangles.

8 Halfway up between the points just sewn and the top of the bauble, sew adjacent open sides together. Hand sew the tassel on the bottom.

Table Centrepiece

Sprays of leaves in black and white can be a year-round table decoration, and as these leaves are glued to chenille stems they can be formed around anything from vases to candles!

What you need

Assorted black and white fabrics: you will need to create about sixty leaf shapes and each requires 3 x 2in (7.5 x 5cm) of fabric

Thirty chenille stems

A handful of polystyrene balls for berries

Hot-glue gun

1 Cut sixty leaf shapes from your fabrics, using the template on page 128. Sew the leaf shapes together in pairs, right sides together, with a ⅛in (3mm) seam allowance.

2 Make a cut in the centre of the back of each leaf, and right along the centre of the length. Cut away the excess fabric at the points.

3 Turn the leaves right sides out through the slit in the back, and press.

4 Topstitch around the edge of each leaf and sew a central vein.

5 Drizzle hot glue along the slit of one leaf at a time, and place the chenille stalk on top before the glue dries – don't let the tip of the stalk be seen from the front of the leaf.

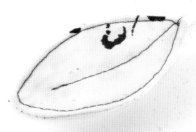

6 When you've completed all the leaves, take half of them, and twist the stalks together to form a spray. Twist the remaining stalks along the main stem.

7 Hot glue the polystyrene balls to the stalk in bunches, as shown left.

Tip

Make up a bunch of leaves in red, and you have a poinsettia! I wrapped a strip of ribbon around the stems and added a bow, then hot glued a few beads to the centre.

Potted Tree Decoration

This elegant tree will add a touch of Christmas class to your home, and the best thing is, it won't shed needles everywhere!

What you need

Four triangles of fabric measuring 18in (46cm) tall and 7in (18cm) across the bottom

About 10½oz (300g) of toy stuffing

A length of ¼in (0.5cm) dowelling, 14in (35.5cm) long

A plant pot: mine is 5in (13cm) tall and 4in (10cm) across

Black spray paint

Air-drying clay

Polystyrene balls

28in (71cm) of chain or beads to decorate

Self-adhesive gems

1 yard (91.5cm) of ¼in (0.5cm) wide silver ribbon

Double-sided craft tape pen

Clear liquid craft glue

1 Spray paint the dowelling and plant pot with black paint.

2 When the paint is dry, push a handful of clay into the pot, filling to about 1in (2.5cm) from the top.

3 Whilst the clay is still soft, push the dowelling straight into the centre, making sure it doesn't lean. Leave the clay to dry.

4 Using your tape pen, roll the sticky adhesive along the ribbon, then wind the ribbon around the dowelling, and around the pot. You could use wet glue for this, but the tape helps to stop the ribbon slipping.

5 Fill the top of the pot with polystyrene balls, and drizzle clear liquid glue over the top to hold them in place. Put to one side to dry.

6 Place two of the triangles right sides together, and sew all the way round, leaving a gap in the centre of the base of about 4in (10cm) for turning through.

7 Snip away the seam allowance at the corners, turn right sides out and press.

8 Repeat steps 6 and 7 for the second pair of triangles. Press the two triangles in half lengthways. Lay one on top of the other, and sew straight down this centre crease line.

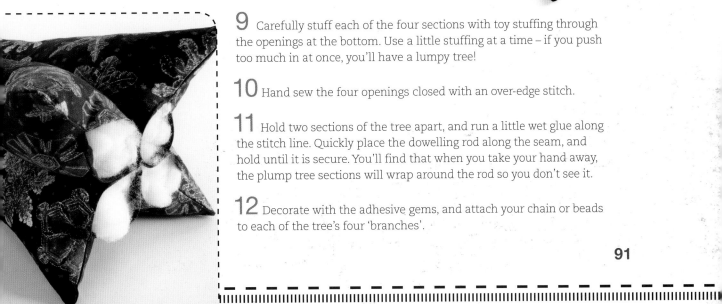

9 Carefully stuff each of the four sections with toy stuffing through the openings at the bottom. Use a little stuffing at a time – if you push too much in at once, you'll have a lumpy tree!

10 Hand sew the four openings closed with an over-edge stitch.

11 Hold two sections of the tree apart, and run a little wet glue along the stitch line. Quickly place the dowelling rod along the seam, and hold until it is secure. You'll find that when you take your hand away, the plump tree sections will wrap around the rod so you don't see it.

12 Decorate with the adhesive gems, and attach your chain or beads to each of the tree's four 'branches'.

Tablemat

I've kept this tablemat quite plain so that my centrepiece will stand out – the mitred corners give a professional finish, and the red embroidery thread woven through a ladder stitch adds just a pop of colour. Make it any size you like: a smaller version would make a useful sewing-machine mat!

What you need

One piece of black fabric measuring 18 x 34in (46 x 86.5cm)

Two strips of striped fabric measuring 42 x 3in (107 x 7.5cm)

Two strips of striped fabric measuring 26 x 3in (66 x 7.5cm)

One piece of backing fabric: I used the same black fabric, measuring 40 x 24in (102 x 61cm)

One piece of thermal wadding (batting) measuring 40 x 24in (102 x 61cm)

3¾ yards (3.4m) of 1in (2.5cm) bias binding

Ruler and pencil

Red embroidery thread and blunt needle

1 Pin one long strip of striped fabric centrally, right sides together, to one long edge of the black rectangle. You will have 4in (10cm) spare at each end.

2 Starting ¼in (0.5cm) from where the black fabric starts, sew together, and finish your stitching ¼in (0.5cm) from the other end of the black fabric.

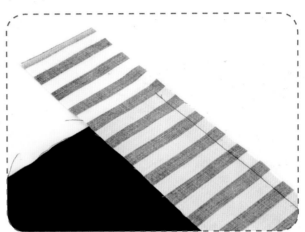

3 Repeat with the remaining three sides of the black fabric and their corresponding strips of striped fabric, making sure that your stitches meet, but don't overlap, in each corner; press.

4 Fold two corner sides together to create a 45-degree angle. Pin the fabric pieces together. If you are using a striped fabric, try to match the stripes to make a chevron effect – you may have to trim your black fabric slightly to achieve this.

5 Using a ruler and pencil, extend the fold of the fabric across the striped fabric and draw a line.

6 Sew along the line, trim away the excess striped fabric and press. Repeat with the next three sides.

7 Using the widest ladder stitch on your machine, sew all the way around the edge of the black fabric. Then take the red embroidery thread, doubled, and weave in and out of the stitches, starting and finishing on the back of the fabric. A blunt needle or bodkin is useful so as not to catch the fabric when weaving. If you don't have either, push the eye end of the needle through the stitches first, but be careful not to prick your finger on the sharp end!

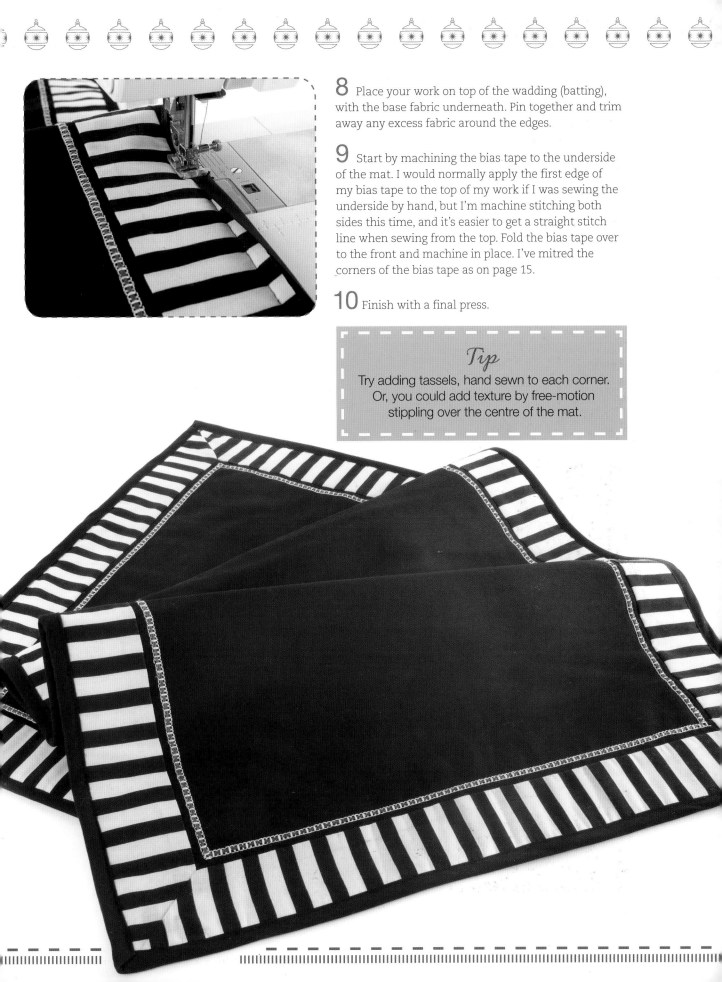

8 Place your work on top of the wadding (batting), with the base fabric underneath. Pin together and trim away any excess fabric around the edges.

9 Start by machining the bias tape to the underside of the mat. I would normally apply the first edge of my bias tape to the top of my work if I was sewing the underside by hand, but I'm machine stitching both sides this time, and it's easier to get a straight stitch line when sewing from the top. Fold the bias tape over to the front and machine in place. I've mitred the corners of the bias tape as on page 15.

10 Finish with a final press.

Tip

Try adding tassels, hand sewn to each corner. Or, you could add texture by free-motion stippling over the centre of the mat.

Kids' Christmas

These character-filled projects will be so much fun for children, and the young at heart! I've chosen to work with felt as it is such a great fabric: it doesn't fray, it is soft to touch and it is perfect to show off your hand sewing skills. These easy projects are a great starting point for a young sewer, and could all be made without using a sewing machine.

Santa Hat Chair Slip

These huge hats will not only cheer up the Christmas table, they are an ideal way to disguise mismatched chairs. Coordinate with Santa placemats and place names, then make smaller ones for your guests to wear! Felt doesn't fray so there's no need to worry about hemming.

What you need

Per hat:

Two pieces of red felt – they should measure 18in (46cm) tall, and the width should be the width of your chair back plus 1in (2.5cm); here I used a 20in (51cm) width

White faux fur – the height should be 8in (20.5cm), and the width should be twice the width of your red felt piece plus ½in (1cm); here I used a 40½in (103cm) width

One ball of white yarn to make the pompom

Card to make a form for the pompom

Three rectangles of green felt measuring 4 x 2in (10 x 5cm)

Two red buttons for the berries

1 From the bottom of the felt, measure and mark 8in (20.5cm) up on each side.

2 Fold the piece in half lengthways. Draw from these side marks to the central fold, on each half, to make a point.

3 Cut along these lines. Repeat with your second piece of felt.

4 Place your two cut pieces of felt together. Sew along the sides and the point to join the front and back together, leaving the bottom edge unstitched. There is no need to turn the piece inside out, as it's nice to see the stitching. Trim the seam allowance with pinking shears if you like, to give a decorative effect.

5 Pin your faux fur around the red felt hat, right sides together and about 3in (7.5cm) up from the bottom edge, before sewing all the way around the bottom edge. If your fur frays a little, use a zigzag stitch on your sewing machine.

6 Fold the fur down and tuck it underneath the edge of the hat; hand sew in place.

7 Take the green felt rectangles and fold them in half lengthways.

8 Draw four curves as shown, starting and ending on the fold, to make the holly-leaf shape.

9 Cut out the shape from all three felt pieces.

10 Arrange the leaves on the hat, to one side, and backstitch down the centre.

11 Add the buttons for berries.

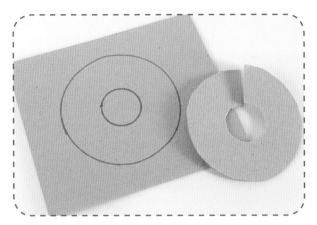

12 To make your pompom, cut two circles of card, measuring 4in (10cm) across.

13 Cut a circular hole in the centre of each, measuring 1½in (4cm) across, then make a cut from the edge in to the centre.

14 Place the two circles together, and begin to wind the yarn around the hoop. The gap you've cut will make it easier to wind the yarn round.

15 When the card is full, hold the centre tightly with one hand, and snip around the edge of the yarn, in between the two discs.

16 Take a length of yarn and feed it in between the two card discs. Knot it tightly. Remove the card.

17 Use this piece of yarn to sew the pompom onto the hat, using a large-eyed needle.

Felt Gift Bags

The children will love to both make and receive these little felt bags, which can be decorated with any Christmassy character you like!

What you need

Per bag:

Two squares of red felt measuring 6 x 6in (15.5 x 15.5cm)

Three rectangles of red felt measuring 6 x 3in (15.5 x 7.5cm)

A length of gingham ribbon measuring ½in (1cm) wide and 16in (41cm) long

Black, red and white embroidery thread split into strands of three

For the snowman:

One 4in (10cm) square of white felt

One 3in (7.5cm) square of black felt

Two small black buttons

Scrap of orange felt

Blusher (optional)

1 Cut a curve from one corner of the white felt to shape the snowman's head. Cut out the hat from black felt and the carrot-shaped nose from orange felt using the templates on page 128.

2 Blanket stitch the white felt piece to the bottom corner of one of your red squares.

3 Straight stitch the hat and nose in place, as shown. Add the buttons for eyes, then backstitch a smile! I've added a touch of blusher on his cheek too, to give him a rosy glow

4 Blanket stitch the sides and bottom to the front.

5 Blanket stitch the back and sides together, and the sides to the base.

6 Line up the top of the front and back of the bag, tucking in the sides.

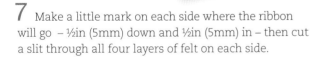

7 Make a little mark on each side where the ribbon will go – ½in (5mm) down and ½in (5mm) in – then cut a slit through all four layers of felt on each side.

8 Thread the ribbon through all four layers on the right-hand side, then pass it through all four layers on the left-hand side. Stitch or glue the ends together to create one continuous handle.

9 When you pull, the bag will close!

Robin Bunting

These cheeky little robins are simple and fun to make – string them along a cord to make birdy bunting, or hang them individually from the tree.

1 First make your template. Draw a 3in (7.5cm) circle, then overlap a 2in (5cm) circle. I used a circle template, but lids would work well.

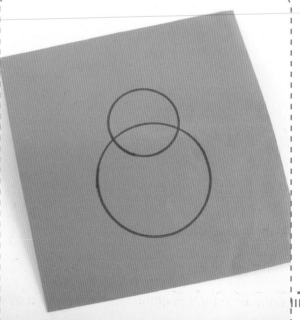

What you need

Per robin:

Two 4in (10cm) squares of light brown felt

One 1½in (4cm) circle of red felt, cut with pinking shears

Two strips of dark brown felt for the legs, measuring about 2 x ⅛in (5cm x 3mm) each

Two pieces of dark brown felt for wings, measuring 2 x ½in (5 x 1cm)

A tiny orange triangle of felt for the beak

Red and black embroidery thread

Card and a pen to make a template

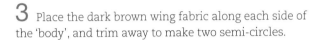

2 Cut two pieces of light brown felt from this shape.

3 Place the dark brown wing fabric along each side of the 'body', and trim away to make two semi-circles.

4 Place the red circle on the tummy of one body piece and hand sew around the edge.

5 Sew the wings on either side with red thread.

6 The beak is attached with two black straight stitches that make nostrils, and the eyes are black French knots (see page 14).

7 Sew the front piece to the back piece of light brown felt with blanket stitch, trapping the legs in place as you go. If you're making a tree hanging, add a loop of thread to the head at this point.

8 Make as many as you like! Sew red embroidery thread across the back of each to string them together – this will stop them twisting.

Tip
The robin's body template could easily be turned into a snowman!

Santa Hat

This is a smaller version of the Santa hat chair slip and will bring a smile to the children's faces!

What you need

Two rectangles of red felt measuring 11 x 13in (28 x 33cm)

A strip of white faux fur measuring 4 x 24in (10 x 61cm)

White yarn for a pompom

Three rectangles of green felt measuring 4 x 2in (10 x 5cm)

Three red buttons for berries

1 Measure and mark each of the long sides of the red felt, 2in (5cm) up from the bottom.

2 Join these marks at the centre top to make a point, and cut. Do this with both pieces of red felt.

3 Place the two pieces of felt together. Sew up both sides of the hat. There is no need to turn right sides out. Place the faux fur, furry side down, across the hat, 2in (5cm) up from the bottom, and sew around the bottom edge. Overlap the ends slightly.

4 Fold the fur fabric down over the edge of the felt and hand sew on the inside.

5 Cut out the holly leaves as for the Santa hat chair slip (see page 100), and backstitch them onto the front right of the hat, adding the buttons for berries.

6 Make the pompom as per the instructions on page 101, and hand stitch it to the point of your hat.

Tip
Have fun with colours and make hats in less traditional pink, green, yellow or blue!

Contemporary Christmas

Bright white and simple green give a modern, fresh look to the Christmas dining room. I've themed the projects around ribbon, triangular trees and free-motion embroidery. Free-motion embroidery is a way of 'doodling' with the needle and thread on your sewing machine. You'll need a free-motion or darning foot. Drop the feed dogs from under the fabric, choose a straight stitch, then simply move the fabric in any direction to create patterns. The quicker you move the fabric, the longer the stitch will be. Don't worry about being accurate, just have fun!

Paper Bag Favours

This is such a simple idea and is a little bit of fun at the dinner table. I've used gift wrap here, but brown wrapping paper would work just as well. Simply rip open the paper pouches to reveal the surprise inside! I'd suggest sweets that don't melt, so avoid chocolate.

What you need

For each favour:
Two pieces of paper measuring 2in (5cm) square
A handful of sweeties

1 Put the two pieces of paper together and sew around three sides.

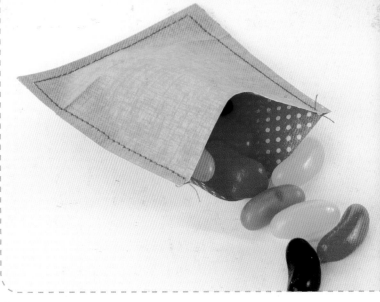

2 Pop your sweeties inside, but don't overfill.

3 Fold the open end so that the seams meet and sew across the top. Leave a few inches of thread at the end of your stitch line for hanging.

4 Make up a few and hang on the tree. Tear open when it comes to treat time!

Tip

You could write your guests' names on the favours, or pop a little written message inside before sewing together. Also, try different shapes, like circles, or try triangles to make paper Christmas trees.

Card Holder

Decorate your walls with the cards you receive with these pretty card holders, and after Christmas why not display the family photographs? I've used double-sided fusible wadding (batting) to stiffen my fabric, but don't iron it until you've finished! You could use a medium-weight interfacing instead.

What you need

For the tails:

Two strips of fabric measuring 36 x 4in (91.5 x 10cm)

Two strips of fabric measuring 32 x 4in (81.5 x 10cm)

Two strips of fabric measuring 28 x 4in (71 x 10cm)

Three strips of double-sided fusible wadding (batting), cut to the same size as the fabric

Three lengths of ½in (1cm) wide ribbon, measuring 36in (91.5cm), 32in (81.5cm) and 28in (71cm) in length

About fifteen small buttons

For the bows:

Three pieces of fabric measuring 16 x 9½in (41 x 24cm)

Three pieces of double-sided fusible wadding (batting) measuring 7½ x 9½in (19 x 24cm)

Three large buttons

Three small curtain rings

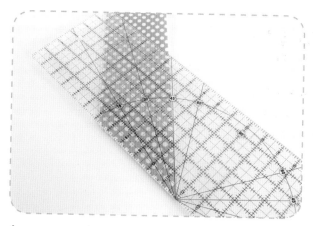

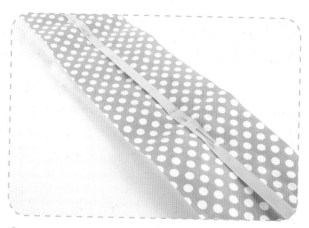

1 Take the first two strips of fabric – wrong sides together – and lay them on top of a corresponding piece of wadding (batting). Cut a 45-degree angle from the bottom of the strips – I find using a rectangular ruler makes it easier. Remove the lower piece of fabric.

2 Pin the corresponding piece of ribbon to the centre of the tail, then sew it in place at intervals of 5–6in (13–15.5cm) – make some gaps larger or smaller to accommodate different sizes of cards.

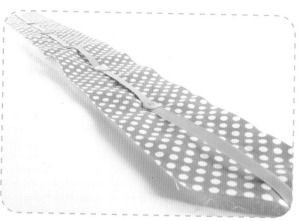

3 Sew a small button on top of each set of stitches.

4 Place the lower piece of fabric you removed in step 1 on top, right sides facing, and sew around three sides, leaving the top open for turning. Make sure you back-tack at the start and finish of your sewing to stop the stitches from coming undone.

5 Snip across the point, then turn the right way out. This is easy to do if you pull on the ribbon.

6 Now press, and the fusible wadding (batting) will adhere.

7 Turn in the open end by about ½in (1cm) and press, before sewing closed with an over-edge stitch.

8 Repeat with the next two tails.

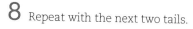

9 Now for the bows! Fold the fabric in half widthways, right sides together, and sew down the open side, leaving a gap of about 3in (7.5cm) in the centre for turning.

10 Manipulate this tube so that the seam sits in the centre of the front, and press open.

11 Place the wadding (batting) on to the side with no seam, and sew across each open end of the tube to secure it.

12 Snip away the excess fabric at the corners and turn right side out.

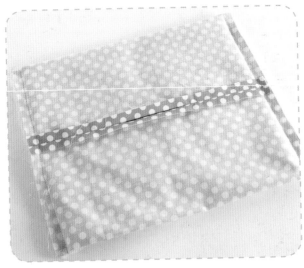

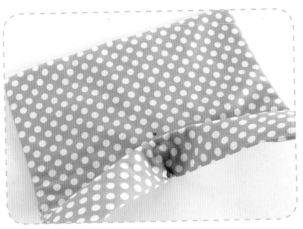

13 Hand sew the opening with ladder stitch, then press. This is when the fusible adhesive will adhere.

14 Turn your piece over so that the seam is underneath. Mark the centre point of the bow's width. Measure halfway down between this centre point and the edge, and pinch up the fabric at this point, as shown, bringing it into the centre and pinning in place.

15 Repeat this process at the top of the bow, pinching halfway between the centre mark and the top edge and pin in place. With your sewing machine, sew a few stitches back and forth across this centre point to secure. Remove the pins.

16 Fold the bow in half along its width, folding the top and bottom sections backwards. Hand sew in the centre at the back – you'll see the fabric fanning out into a lovely bow! Sew the curtain ring on at this point.

17 Sew a large button to the centre front.

18 Repeat steps 9–17 to create two more bows.

19 Hand sew the tails to the back of the bows.

Tip
Decorate your tails with small bows or fabric flowers instead of buttons.

Ribbon Tree Placemats

Add a modern, fresh look to your Christmas dining table with these quilted placemats.

What you need

A circle of white cotton fabric measuring 12in (30.5cm) across: I used a dinner plate as a template

A circle of backing fabric measuring 12in (30.5cm) across

A circle of heat-resistant wadding (batting) measuring 12in (30.5cm) across

38in (96.5cm) of 1in (2.5cm) bias binding

About 30in (76cm) of green ribbon in varying tones and widths

Free-motion embroidery foot for your sewing machine

A button or two to decorate the tree

Repositionable spray adhesive

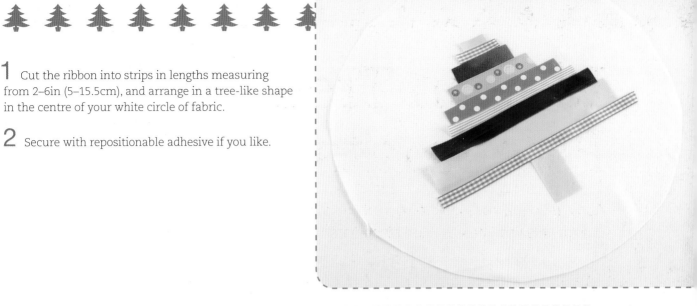

1 Cut the ribbon into strips in lengths measuring from 2–6in (5–15.5cm), and arrange in a tree-like shape in the centre of your white circle of fabric.

2 Secure with repositionable adhesive if you like.

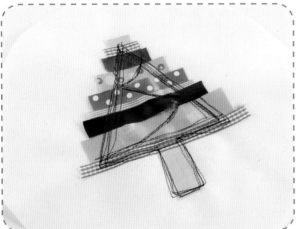

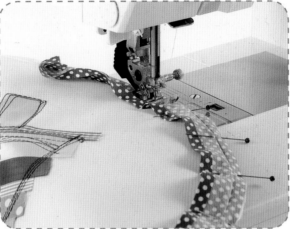

3 Using your embroidery foot and a contrasting coloured thread, sew around the triangular tree a few times. I like the 'scribbly' look of uneven lines, so don't worry if you're not sewing straight!

4 Lay this piece right side up on top of the heat-resistant wadding (batting) and then the backing fabric, right side down, using a light spray of repositionable spray adhesive to hold together.

5 Apply the bias binding all around the edge (see page 15).

6 Put your embroidery foot back on your machine and, using white thread, 'draw' all over the background of the mat, avoiding the bias tape and ribbon tree. I'm certainly no quilter, but there are no rules here – go around in circles or triangles, or both! Add a button or two to the top of the tree.

Christmas Tree Table Runner

Ideal for any Christmas table, this pretty runner will coordinate with your contemporary Christmas décor, and is practical too, as it is padded with thermal wadding (batting) to help protect your table from heat damage.

What you need

½ yard (46cm) of white cotton fabric: mine is the width of the roll, which is 54in (137cm)

Backing fabric measuring the same as your white cotton fabric

Thermal wadding (batting) measuring the same as your white cotton fabric

Nine triangles of fabric, in various sizes of approximately 5 x 8in (13 x 20.5cm)

Nine small pieces of fabric cut into 'pot' shapes

Up to nine pieces of fabric cut into circles or star shapes for the tops of the trees

A few circles of fabric for baubles

4 yards (3.6m) of 1in (2.5cm) bias binding

Repositionable spray fabric adhesive

Free-motion embroidery foot for your sewing machine

1 Arrange the triangle trees evenly across the white fabric, every other one upside down, with the pots at the bottom and the stars or circles on top. Place a few baubles here and there on top of some of the trees. Secure all the pieces with a little spray adhesive.

2 Take to your sewing machine, and free-motion stitch in a contrasting colour around each tree, pot, star and bauble. Go around a few times, and don't worry if your stitch lines aren't straight! You might want to embroider some extra baubles on as well.

3 Lay this topper over the thermal wadding (batting), then over the backing fabric. Spray again to secure, and add a few pins if you like.

4 Change to white thread and free-motion embroider all over the white fabric, avoiding the trees. I've just doodled in circles and triangles with no particular pattern. You can see what a difference it makes in the photograph, as opposed to leaving the fabric plain.

5 Continue until the whole runner is embroidered.

6 Trim the edges of the runner if you find that the wadding (batting) has 'grown'.

7 Apply the bias tape all around the edge of your runner to finish, see page 15.

Bottle Cooler

By using insulated wadding (batting) you'll help to keep your cold drinks chilled, and this made-to-measure cosy will create a best-dressed bottle for the Christmas table!

What you need

Per bottle cooler:

One piece of fabric – the size will depend on the size of your bottle, see step 1 for calculations

One piece of lining fabric measuring the same

One piece of insulated wadding (batting) measuring the same

A length of ribbon measuring 15in (38cm)

Ruler and pencil

1 First measure the height of your bottle and add 2in (5cm), then the circumference, and add another 2in (5cm). My bottle measures 13 x 12in (33 x 30.5cm) so my fabric measures 15 x 14in (38 x 35.5cm). Cut one piece of outer fabric, one of lining and one of wadding (batting) to your measurements.

2 Take your rectangles of fabric, wadding (batting) and lining and cut each one in half lengthways.

3 Measure 3in (7.5cm) down from the top of the outer and lining fabrics and mark.

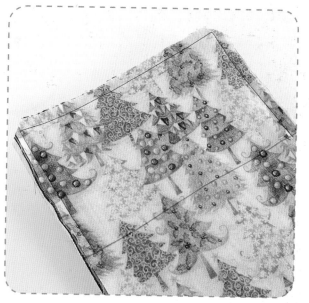

4 Lay one piece of outer fabric and one piece of lining fabric right sides together, with a piece of wadding (batting) underneath; pin. Sew around the top: start at your mark on one side, sew up to the top, across the top and back down, stopping at the mark on the opposite side. Repeat with the second set of fabrics. Snip across the corners of the seam allowance.

5 Now place the outer pieces of the bottom sections of the bag right sides together and sew.

6 Do the same with the lining pieces, but this time leave a 4in (10cm) gap in one side for turning. Try to make sure that your stitches meet at the point where the bottom section meets the top, without overlapping.

7 To make the base of the bag square, fold the base seam to meet the side seams and sew across, 1in (2.5cm) from the point. See 'making a bag base' on page 16. Repeat with the lining.

8 Turn the whole piece right side out and press. Sew your turning gap closed then push the lining into the bag base.

9 Fold the ribbon in half and sew onto the side seam just below the opening. Pop in a chilled bottle. Cheers!

Tip

When your bottle is in transit, leave the collar up to help protect it.

Ribbon Tree Wall Hanging

If there's no room in your home for a real tree, why not decorate the wall with this ribbon tree picture!

1 Draw a triangle in the centre of one white piece of fabric measuring 9in (23cm) tall and 8in (20.5cm) across the bottom.

2 Using a large dinner plate as a template, draw four evenly spaced curves up the tree – this is where you'll sew your ribbon.

Tip

If you don't want to frame your finished piece, you could just sew the ribbon lengths to a piece of thick fabric and cut around the tree.

3 Cut the ribbon into 6in (15.5cm) lengths.

4 Fold each length of ribbon in half and pin the strips in place along the lowest curved line. Sew across the curved line to secure them.

5 Repeat step 4, working up the curved lines one at a time, until the whole triangle is covered.

6 Make the star by cutting the yellow ribbon into five 4in (10cm) lengths, and two 2in (5cm) lengths. Loop the five longer pieces in half, and join together in a 'flower' shape. Sew the ends together, then sew on the two remaining pieces of ribbon to make 'tails'.

7 Sew the two buttons, one on top of the other, to the centre of the star, then stitch to the top of the tree. Loop the brown ribbon and sew at the base of the tree.

8 Layer the fabric topper over the wadding (batting) and the backing fabric. Pin together. Using white thread, free-motion embroider all over the white fabric, avoiding the tree. I've sewn in triangular shapes as I felt it matched the design of the tree.

9 Add the bias binding, mitring the corners following the steps given on page 15.

10 Sew a small loop of ribbon to the centre back of the picture to hang it by.

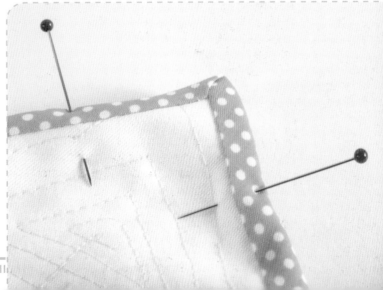

Tree Pictures

These pictures are so quick to make, and I think the simple angular lines against a plain white background make a really striking Christmas artwork! I bought some low-cost white frames, and embroidered fabric straight on to the paper backgrounds. This is an unusual alternative to embroidering on fabric, as you'll find that the paper has a sheen that catches the light. If you can't find white frames, use white spray paint, and embroider onto lightweight white card. A word of warning – this may blunt your needle somewhat!

What you need

8¼ x 11¾in (21 x 29.7cm) white glazed picture frame

A triangle of fabric measuring about 6in (15.5cm) tall and 4in (10cm) across the bottom

A small piece of square fabric for the pot, about 1in (2.5cm) square, trimmed to make a 'pot' shape

Repositionable spray adhesive

Free-motion embroidery foot for your sewing machine

Angelina fibres

1 Carefully remove the backing board and paper from your frame. Leave the glass intact, and try not to get fingerprints on it!

2 Place the triangle of fabric in the centre of the paper, securing with a little spray adhesive.

3 Stick the 'pot' just underneath.

4 Drop your feed dogs and start to sew! Sew around the edges of your fabric, then curving back and forth across the tree to look like a garland. Sew around the pot and create a trunk with stitching. Don't stitch over the same place more than three or four times, as your paper may tear.

5 Lay a few strands of Angelina fibres over the tree, then pop the paper back into its frame.

Tip
If you'd like to decorate your tree further, a few sequins or metallic thread would look stunning. Remember that it will be going behind glass so don't add anything too three-dimensional!

Templates

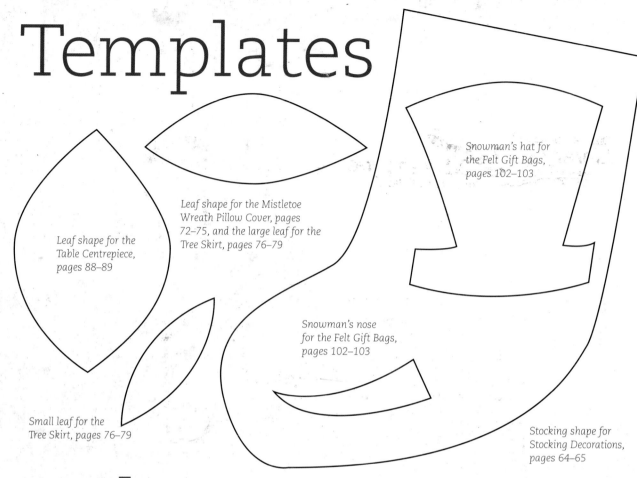

Leaf shape for the Mistletoe Wreath Pillow Cover, pages 72–75, and the large leaf for the Tree Skirt, pages 76–79

Leaf shape for the Table Centrepiece, pages 88–89

Snowman's hat for the Felt Gift Bags, pages 102–103

Snowman's nose for the Felt Gift Bags, pages 102–103

Small leaf for the Tree Skirt, pages 76–79

Stocking shape for Stocking Decorations, pages 64–65

Index